Next-Generation Firewalls

FOR

DUMMIES®

by Lawrence C. Miller, CISSP

D0188285

WILEY

Wiley Publishing, Inc.

Next-Generation Firewalls For Dummies®

Published by
Wiley Publishing, Inc.
111 River Street
Hoboken, NJ 07030-5774

Copyright © 2011 by Wiley Publishing, Inc., Indianapolis, Indiana

Published by Wiley Publishing, Inc., Indianapolis, Indiana

ISBN: 978-0-470-93955-0

Manufactured in the United States of America

10 9 8 7 6 5 4 3 2

Publisher's Acknowledgments
For general information on our other products and services, please contact our Business Development Department in the U.S. at 317-572-3205. For details on how to create a custom For Dummies book for your business or organization, contact info@dummies.biz. For information about licensing the For Dummies brand for products or services, contact BrandedRights&Licenses@Wiley.com.

Acquistions, Editorial, and Media Development

Senior Project Editor: Zoë Wykes
Editorial Manager: Rev Mengle
Business Development Representative: Karen Hattan
Custom Publishing Project Specialist: Michael Sullivan

Composition Services

Senior Project Coordinator: Kristie Rees
Layout and Graphics: Carl Byers, Carrie A. Cesavice, Cheryl Grubbs
Proofreader: Rebecca Denoncour
Special Help from Palo Alto Networks: Chris King

WILEY

Table of Contents

Introduction

● ●

*W*ith new Internet-based threats being launched faster than ever and increasingly targeting "firewall friendly" applications and application-layer vulnerabilities, traditional firewalls are becoming less and less capable of adequately protecting corporate networks.

The rapid evolution of applications and threats, coupled with the relative stagnation of traditional security technologies, has resulted in a loss of visibility and control for IT organizations attempting to keep their enterprises secure.

Despite their best efforts to restore application visibility and control, and regain the advantage in protecting their networks and information assets, most organizations remain stymied. Lacking a truly innovative solution, they turn to specialized single-purpose security appliances that fail to fully address today's security challenges, and are not part of a comprehensive security strategy.

The resulting appliance sprawl is costly and complex — characteristics that are never desirable in a solution. But in today's tough economic climate when organizations must do more with less — both money and IT staff — complex and costly fixes are entirely unacceptable.

Instead, an entirely new and innovative approach to network security is needed — it's time to reinvent the firewall!

About This Book

This book provides an in-depth overview of next-generation firewalls. It examines the evolution of network security, the rise of Enterprise 2.0 applications and their associated threats, the shortcomings of traditional firewalls, and the advanced capabilities found in next-generation firewalls.

Foolish Assumptions

This book assumes you have a working knowledge of network security. As such, it is written primarily for technical readers who are evaluating potential new solutions to address their organizations' security challenges.

How This Book Is Organized

This book consists of six short chapters and an appendix. Here's a brief synopsis of the chapters to pique your curiosity!

Chapter 1: Understanding the Evolution of Network Security

We begin with a look at the role that firewalls traditionally play in network security, as well as some of the challenges of network security today.

Chapter 2: Defining the Application and Threat Landscape

Chapter 2 describes several trends affecting application development and their usage in enterprises. You find out about the business benefits, as well as the security risks associated with various applications, and how new threats are exploiting "accessibility features" in Enterprise 2.0 applications.

Chapter 3: Recognizing the Challenges of Legacy Security Infrastructures

Chapter 3 explains why traditional port-based firewalls and intrusion prevention systems are inadequate for protecting enterprises against new and emerging threats.

Chapter 4: Solving the Problem with Next-Generation Firewalls

Chapter 4 takes a deep dive into the advanced features and capabilities of next-generation firewalls. You learn what a next-generation firewall is, what it isn't, and how it can benefit your organization.

Chapter 5: Deploying Next-Generation Firewalls

Chapter 5 explains the importance of security policies and controls, and the role of next-generation firewalls in implementing those policies and controls. You also get some help defining specific technical requirements for your organization, and planning the deployment of a next-generation firewall on your network.

Chapter 6: Ten Evaluation Criteria for Next-Generation Firewalls

Here, in that familiar *For Dummies* Part of Tens format, we present ten features to look for and criteria to consider when choosing a next-generation firewall.

Glossary

And, just in case you get stumped on a technical term or abbreviation here or there, we include a glossary to help you sort through it all!

Icons Used in This Book

Throughout this book, we occasionally use icons to call attention to important information that is particularly worth noting. Sadly, James Dean (the pop icon, not the sausage guy) isn't available to point this information out for you, so we do it instead!

 This icon points out information or a concept that may well be worth committing to memory, so don't make like a wise guy and fuggedaboutit — instead, make wise and don't ever forget it!

 You won't find a map of the human genome or the secret to cold fusion here (or maybe you will, hmm), but if you're seeking to attain the seventh level of NERD-vana, take note! This icon explains the jargon beneath the jargon.

 Thank you for reading, hope you enjoy the book, please take care of your writers. Seriously, this icon points out helpful suggestions and useful nuggets of information that may just save you some time and headaches.

 The Surgeon General has determined . . . well okay, it's actually nothing _that_ hazardous. Still, this icon points out potential pitfalls and easily confused concepts.

Where to Go from Here

It's been said that a journey of a thousand miles begins with a single step. Well, at 72 pages, reading this book is more like a quick — but informative — jaunt across your living room!

Don't worry about missing the plot, or spoiling the ending. Each chapter in this book is written to stand on its own, so feel free to start wherever you'd like and jump ahead to the chapters that interest you most. Of course, if you're a little more of a traditionalist, you could just turn the page and start at the beginning!

Chapter 1

Understanding the Evolution of Network Security

In This Chapter

▶ Understanding why port-based firewalls have become obsolete

▶ Addressing the data leakage problem

▶ Achieving regulatory compliance

*J*ust as antivirus software has been a cornerstone of PC security since the early days of the Internet, firewalls have been the cornerstone of network security.

Today's application and threat landscape renders traditional port-based firewalls largely ineffective at protecting corporate networks and sensitive data. Applications are the conduit through which everything flows — a vector for our business and personal lives — along with their associated benefits and risks. Such risks include new and emerging threats, data leakage, and noncompliance.

This chapter explains how traditional firewalls operate, why they cannot meet today's application and threat challenges, and how data leakage and compliance issues are defining network security and the need for a better firewall.

Why Legacy Firewalls Are No Longer Effective

A firewall, at its most basic level, controls traffic flow between a trusted network (such as a corporate LAN) and an untrusted or public network (such as the Internet). The most commonly deployed firewalls today are port-based (or packet filtering) firewalls, or some variation (such as stateful inspection) of this basic type of firewall. These firewalls are popular because they are relatively simple to operate and maintain, generally inexpensive, have good throughput, and have been the prevalent design for more than two decades.

In the rapid pace of the Internet Age, nearly two decades means the basic technology behind port-based firewalls is medieval. In fact, network security is often likened to the Dark Ages — a network perimeter is analogous to the walls of a castle, with a firewall controlling access — like a drawbridge. And like a drawbridge that is either up or down, a port-based firewall is limited to just two options for controlling network traffic: allow or block.

Port-based firewalls (and their variants) use source/destination IP addresses and TCP/UDP port information to determine whether or not a packet should be allowed to pass between networks or network segments. The firewall inspects the first few bytes of the TCP header in an IP packet to determine the application protocol — for example, SMTP (port 25), and HTTP (port 80).

Most firewalls are configured to allow all traffic originating from the trusted network to pass through to the untrusted network, unless it is explicitly blocked by a rule. For example, the Simple Network Management Protocol (SNMP) might be explicitly blocked to prevent certain network information from being inadvertently transmitted to the Internet. This would be accomplished by blocking UDP ports 161 and 162, regardless of the source or destination IP address.

Static port control is relatively easy. Stateful inspection firewalls address *dynamic* applications that use more than one well-defined port (such as FTP ports 20 and 21). When a computer or server on the trusted network originates a session with a computer or server on the untrusted network, a connection is established. On stateful packet inspection firewalls, a dynamic rule is temporarily created to allow responses or replies from the computer or server on the untrusted network. Otherwise, return traffic needs to be explicitly permitted, or access rules need to be manually created on the firewall (which usually isn't practical).

All of this works well as long as everyone plays by the rules. Unfortunately, the rules are more like guidelines and not everyone using the Internet is nice!

The Internet now accounts for the majority of traffic traversing enterprise networks. And it's not just Web surfing. The Internet has spawned a new generation of applications being accessed by network users for both personal and business use. Many of these applications help improve user and business productivity, while other applications consume large amounts of bandwidth, pose needless security risks, and increase business liabilities — for example, data leaks and compliance — both of which are addressed in the following sections. And many of these applications incorporate "accessibility" techniques, such as using nonstandard ports, port-hopping, and tunneling, to evade traditional port-based firewalls.

IT organizations have tried to compensate for deficiencies in traditional port-based firewalls by surrounding them with proxies, intrusion prevention systems, URL filtering, and other costly and complex devices, all of which are equally ineffective in today's application and threat landscape.

Data Leakage Is a Problem

Large scale, public exposures of sensitive or private data are far too common. Numerous examples of accidental and deliberate data leakage continue to regularly make nightmare headlines, exposing the loss of tens of thousands of credit card numbers by a major retailer, or social security numbers leaking by a government agency, health care organization, or employer. For example, in December 2008, an improperly configured and *prohibited* peer-to-peer (P2P) file sharing application exposed a database of 24,000 U.S. Army soldiers' personal information to the public domain. Unfortunately, such incidents are not isolated: the U.S. Army's Walter Reed Medical Center, a U.S. Government contractor working on Marine One, and Pfizer Corporation all had earlier high-profile breaches of a similar nature. In all of these cases, sensitive data was leaked via an application that was expressly prohibited by policy but not adequately enforced with technology.

Data leakage prevention (DLP) technologies are being touted as a panacea and have captured the attention of many IT organizations. Unfortunately, given the scope, size, and distributed nature of most enterprise datasets, just discovering where the data is and who owns it is an insurmountable challenge. Adding to this challenge, questions regarding access control, reporting, data classification, data at-rest versus data in-transit, desktop and server agents, and encryption abound. As a result, many DLP initiatives within organizations progress slowly and eventually falter.

Many data loss prevention solutions attempt to incorporate too much of the information security function (and even include elements of storage management!) into an already unwieldy offering. Needless to say, this broadened scope adds complexity, time, and expense — both in hard costs and in staff time. Thus, DLP technologies are often cumbersome, ironically incomplete (focusing mostly on the Web and e-mail), and for many organizations — overkill . . . not to mention expensive!

Furthermore, many of the recent breaches caused by unauthorized and improperly configured P2P file sharing applications wouldn't have been prevented by the typical implementation of DLP technologies on the market today — because control of applications isn't addressed.

Some organizations will have to go through the effort of a large-scale DLP implementation — which should include data discovery, classification, and cataloging. But for most organizations, controlling the applications most often used to leak sensitive data and stopping unauthorized transmission of private or sensitive data, such as credit card and social security numbers, is all that is needed. Exerting that control at trust boundaries (the network perimeter) is ideal — whether the demarcation point is between inside and outside or internal users and internal resources in the datacenter. The firewall sits in the perfect location, seeing all traffic traversing different networks and network segments. Unfortunately, legacy port- and protocol-based firewalls can't do anything about any of this — being ignorant of applications, users, and content. To effectively address data leakage with a firewall solution, organizations should

- ✔ Gain control over the applications on their network — thus limiting the avenues of data leakage
- ✔ Scan the applications they do want on their networks, for sensitive or private data
- ✔ Understand which users are initiating these application transactions and why
- ✔ Implement appropriate control policies and technology to prevent accidental or intentional data leakage

If enterprises could control the flow of sensitive or private data at the perimeter, many of the data loss incidents that regularly make the news could be avoided. Unfortunately, legacy security infrastructures, with traditional firewalls as the cornerstone, are ill-equipped to provide this functionality.

Compliance Is Not Optional

With more than 400 regulations worldwide mandating information security and data protection requirements, organizations everywhere are struggling to attain and maintain compliance. Examples of these regulations include HIPAA, FISMA, FINRA, and GLBA in the U.S., and the EU Data Protection Act (DPA) in Europe.

Ironically, perhaps the most far-reaching, most effective, and best-known compliance requirement today isn't even a government regulation. The Payment Card Industry Data Security Standard (PCI DSS) was created by the major payment card brands (American Express, MasterCard, Visa, and others) to protect companies, banks, and consumers from identity theft and fraudulent card use. And as economies rely more and more on payment card transactions, the risks of lost cardholder data will only increase, making any effort to protect the data critical — whether compliance-driven or otherwise.

PCI DSS is applicable to any business that transmits, processes, or stores payment cards (such as credit cards or debit cards), regardless of the number or amount of transactions processed.

Companies that do not comply can be subject to stiff penalties including fines of up to $25,000 per month for minor violations, fines of up to $500,000 for violations that result in actual lost or stolen financial data, and loss of card-processing authorization (making it almost impossible for a business to operate).

While compliance requirements are almost entirely based on information-security best practices, it is important to remember that security and compliance aren't the same thing. Regardless of whether or not a business is PCI compliant, a data breach can be very costly. According to research conducted by Forrester, the estimated *per record* cost of a breach (including fines, cleanup, lost opportunities, and other costs) ranges from $90 (for a low profile, nonregulated company) to $305 (for a high-profile, highly regulated company).

Security and compliance are related, but they are not the same thing!

PCI DSS version 1.2 consists of 12 general requirements and more than 200 specific requirements. Of the 12 general requirements, the following specifically address firewall and firewall-related requirements:

- ✔ **Requirement 1:** Install and maintain a firewall configuration to protect cardholder data.

- ✔ **Requirement 5:** Use and regularly update anti-virus software or programs.

- ✔ **Requirement 6:** Develop and maintain secure systems and applications.

- ✔ **Requirement 7:** Restrict access to cardholder data by business need-to-know.

- ✔ **Requirement 10:** Track and monitor all access to network resources and cardholder data.

- ✔ **Appendix F:** To use network segmentation to reduce PCI DSS scope, an entity must isolate systems that store, process, or transmit cardholder data from the rest of the network.

Chapter 2

Defining the Application and Threat Landscape

∙ ∙

In This Chapter

▶ Identifying applications as good, bad, or good and bad

▶ Understanding accessibility tactics

▶ Recognizing the speed and sophistication of today's threats

∙ ∙

*N*etwork security used to be relatively simple — everything was more or less black and white — either clearly bad or clearly good. Business applications constituted good traffic that should be allowed, while pretty much everything else constituted bad traffic that should be blocked.

Problems with this approach today include the fact that applications have become

➤ Increasingly "gray" — classifying types of applications as good or bad is not a straightforward exercise.

➤ Increasingly evasive.

➤ The predominant vector of today's cybercriminals and threat developers.

This chapter explores the evolving application and threat landscape, the blurring distinction between user- and business-applications, and the strategic nature of many of these applications (and their associated risks) for businesses today.

Applications Are Not All Good or All Bad

Over the past decade, the application landscape has changed dramatically for organizations. Corporate productivity applications have been joined by a plethora of personal and consumer-oriented applications. This convergence of corporate infrastructures and personal technologies is being driven by a trend known as *consumerization* which, according to Gartner, will be the most significant trend affecting IT through 2015.

The process of consumerization occurs as users increasingly find personal technology and applications that are more powerful or capable, more convenient, less expensive, quicker to install, and easier to use, than corporate IT solutions. These user-centric "lifestyle" applications and technologies enable individuals to improve their personal efficiency, handle their non-work affairs, and maintain online personas, among other things. Common examples include Google Docs, instant messaging applications, and Web-based e-mail. Enterprise 2.0 applications highlight the dissolution of the traditional distinctions between business and personal use. More often than not, the same applications used for social interaction are being used for work-related purposes. And as the boundary between work and their personal lives becomes less distinct, users are practically demanding that these same tools be available to them in their workplaces.

Catering to this demand, technology vendors and developers enjoy vast economies of scale and the pervasive benefits of viral marketing. Selling small quantities to literally hundreds of millions of individual users, rather than large quantities to relatively few corporate customers means

- ✔ Shorter buying cycles — a purchase is a personal choice rather than a corporate decision.

- ✔ Focusing on functionality and ease of use, rather than standards and interoperability.

- ✔ Constantly and rapidly improving products, based on large-scale and virtually instantaneous user feedback.

The adoption of Enterprise 2.0 applications is being driven by users, not by IT. The ease with which they can be accessed, combined with the fact that today's knowledge workers are accustomed to using them, points toward a continuation of the consumerization trend. Defined by *Appopedia* (www.theapp gap.com) as "a system of web-based technologies that provide rapid and agile collaboration, information sharing, emergence and integration capabilities in the extended enterprise," Enterprise 2.0 applications have taken the world by storm. What started as a few applications that were mostly focused on searching, linking, and tagging, rapidly shifted to a horde of applications that enable authoring, networking, and sharing.

Examples of first-generation Enterprise 2.0 applications include

- Wikis such as Socialtext
- Blogging tools such as Blogger
- RSS tools such as NewsGator
- Enterprise bookmarking and tagging tools such as Cogenz
- Messaging tools such as AOL Instant Messenger (AIM)

Examples of second-generation Enterprise 2.0 applications include

- Content management tools such as SharePoint
- Browser-based file sharing tools such as MegaUpload.com
- Complex social networks such as Facebook
- Publishing tools such as YouTube
- Unified messaging tools such as Skype
- Posting tools such as Twitter and social bookmarking

To gain an appreciation for how rapidly the innovation and adoption cycles have accelerated for these applications, consider the following (based on an analysis of 347 organizations worldwide):

- In less than 18 months since its inception in April 2008, Facebook chat has overtaken Yahoo! IM and AIM inside enterprises, further demonstrating how much stickier Enterprise 2.0 applications are over Enterprise 1.0 applications.
- Between March 2009 and September 2009, the enterprise penetration of Google Docs has increased from 33 percent to 82 percent.

✔ In that same time period, Twitter use in enterprises jumped 252 percent in terms of sessions and 775 percent in terms of bandwidth.

Unsure of how to leverage the consumerization trend in their business processes, many organizations either implicitly allow these personal technologies and Enterprise 2.0 applications by simply ignoring their use in the workplace, or explicitly prohibit their use, but are then unable to effectively enforce such policies with traditional firewalls and security technologies. Neither of these two approaches is ideal, and both incur inherent risks for the organization. In addition to lost productivity, adverse issues for the organization include

✔ Creating a subculture of back-channel or underground workflow processes that are critical to the businesses' operations, but are known only to a few users and fully dependent on personal technologies and applications.

✔ Introducing new risks to the entire networking and computing infrastructure, due to the presence of unknown, and therefore unaddressed and unpatched, vulnerabilities, as well as threats that target normal application and user behavior — whether a vulnerability exists in the application or not.

✔ Being exposed to non-compliance penalties for organizations that are subject to regulatory requirements such as HIPAA, FINRA, and PCI DSS.

✔ Having employees circumvent controls with external proxies, encrypted tunnels, and remote desktop applications, making it difficult, if not impossible, for security and risk managers to see the risks they're attempting to manage.

The challenge is not only the growing diversity of the applications, but also the inability to clearly and consistently classify them as good or bad. Although many are clearly good (low risk, high reward), and others are clearly bad (high risk, low reward), most are somewhere in between. Moreover, the end of the spectrum that these applications fall on can vary from one scenario to the next and from user to user or from session to session.

For example, using a social networking application to share product documentation with a prospective customer would be "good" (medium risk, high reward), while using the same application to forward details of an upcoming release to a "friends list" that includes employees of a competitor would be "not so good" (high risk, no reward).

Indeed, many organizations now use a variety of social networking applications to support a wide range of legitimate business functions, such as recruiting, research and development, marketing, and customer support — and many are even inclined to allow the use of lifestyle applications, to some extent, as a way to provide an "employee friendly" work environment and improve morale.

Enabling Facebook usage while protecting the business

Facebook is rapidly extending its influence from the personal world to the corporate world, as employees use these applications to get their jobs done. At the same time, many organizations are looking at the nearly 500 million Facebook users as an opportunity to conduct research, execute targeted marketing, gather product feedback, and increase awareness. The end result is that Facebook can help organizations improve their bottom line.

However, formally enabling the use of Facebook introduces several challenges to organizations. Many organizations are unaware of how heavily Facebook is being used, or for what purpose. In most cases, policies governing specific usage are nonexistent or unenforceable. Finally, users tend to be too trusting, operating in

a "click now, think later" mentality which introduces significant security risks.

Like any application that is brought into the enterprise by end-users, blindly allowing Facebook may result in propagation of threats, loss of data, and damage to the corporate reputation. Blindly blocking Facebook is also an inappropriate response because it may play an important role in the business and may force users to find alternative means of accessing it (such as proxies, circumvention tools, and others). Organizations should follow a systematic process to develop, enable, and enforce appropriate Facebook usage policies while simultaneously protecting network resources.

(continued)

(continued)

1. **Find out who's using Facebook.** There are many cases where there may already be a "corporate" Facebook presence established by marketing or sales, so it is critical that IT determine which social networking applications are in use, who is using them, and the associated business objectives. By meeting with the business groups and discussing the common company goals, IT can use this step to move away from the image of "always saying no" and towards the role of business enabler.

2. **Develop a corporate Facebook policy.** Once Facebook usage patterns are determined, organizations should engage in discussions regarding what should and should not be said or posted about the company, the competition, and the appropriate language. Educating users on the security risks associated with Facebook is another important element to encouraging usage for business purposes. Organizations need to change the "click now, think later" mentality to a "think now, then click" attitude to better protect both users and the organization from potential threats carried by social networks.

3. **Use technology to monitor and enforce policy.** The outcome of each of these discussions should be documented with an explanation of how IT will apply security policies to safely and securely enable use of Facebook within enterprise environments.

Documenting and enforcing a social networking usage policy can help organizations improve their bottom line while boosting employee morale. An added benefit is that it can help bridge the chasm that commonly exists between the IT department and business groups.

Research from McKinsey and Company and the Association for Information and Image Management (AIIM) shows that companies are seeing measurable benefits from the use of Enterprise 2.0 applications and technologies. Specific benefits include an increased ability to share ideas, more rapid access to knowledge experts, and a reduction in travel, operations, and communications costs. For example, you can now make ticket reservations on Delta Airlines' Facebook page!

Today's network security solutions, therefore, must be able not only to distinguish one type of application from the next, but also to account for other contextual variables surrounding its use and to vary the resulting action that will be taken accordingly.

Applications Are Evasive

Although "distinguishing one type of application from the next" sounds simple, it really isn't — for a number of reasons. In order to maximize their accessibility and use, many applications are designed from the outset to circumvent traditional firewalls, by dynamically adjusting how they communicate. For the end-user, this means an application can be used from anywhere, at anytime. Common tactics include

- ✔ **Port hopping,** where ports/protocols are randomly shifted over the course of a session

- ✔ **Use of non-standard ports,** such as running Yahoo! Messenger over TCP port 80 (HTTP) instead of the standard TCP port for Yahoo! Messenger (5050)

- ✔ **Tunneling within commonly used services,** such as when peer-to-peer (P2P) file sharing or an instant messenger (IM) client like Meebo is running over HTTP

- ✔ **Hiding within SSL encryption,** which masks the application traffic, for example, over TCP port 443 (HTTPS)

The Spring 2010 *Application Usage and Risk Report* by Palo Alto Networks found that out of 741 unique applications analyzed, 65 percent were designed for accessibility using these techniques. Figure 2-1 shows the comparative growth of applications using accessibility features over the past 18 months (covered by three semi-annual *Application Usage and Risk Reports*).

Many standard client-server applications are being redesigned to take advantage of Web technologies. Figure 2-1 shows that 30 percent (149) of the accessibility-focused applications analyzed in the report are client-server-based, a fact that contradicts the notion that "accessible" applications always use the browser. At the same time, enterprises are increasingly embracing cloud-based Web services such as Salesforce.com, WebEx, and Google Apps — which often initiate in a browser but then quickly switch to more client-server behavior (rich client, proprietary transactions, and others).

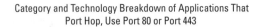

Category and Technology Breakdown of Applications That
Port Hop, Use Port 80 or Port 443

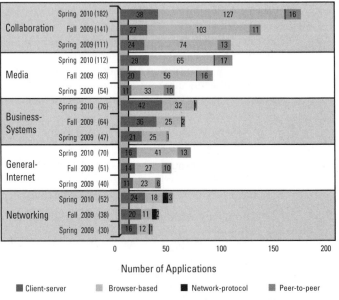

Figure 2-1: Comparative growth of applications with accessibility "features."

Google applications:
The epitome of Enterprise 2.0?

To a certain extent, many of the applications that Google publishes epitomize Enterprise 2.0 (Web 2.0 and Internet-based applications that are used for business purposes). The Spring 2010 *Application Usage and Risk Report* by Palo Alto Networks identifies 22 Google applications that cover a wide functionality spectrum: productivity (Google Docs, Analytics, Calendar), social networking (Orkut), communications (Gmail, Gtalk, Voice) and entertainment (YouTube, Picasa). These applications were found with overwhelming frequency in organizations participating in the study (see the following figure).

When compared to Palo Alto Networks' Fall 2009 *Application Usage and Risk Report,* several facts support the trend toward increased usage of Enterprise 2.0 applications:

✔ Google Docs consumed 55 percent more bandwidth and 42 percent more sessions on a per organization basis.

✔ Google Calendar consumed 18 percent more bandwidth and 30 percent more sessions on a per organization basis.

✔ Bandwidth consumption for Google Talk Gadget shot up by 56 percent while Google Talk dropped 76 percent. Google Talk Gadget is a Flash-based browser plugin that performs the same functions as the client-server—based Google Talk. The most significant difference is the fact that it is browser-based and therefore easier to use in environments where desktop controls restrict application installation by end-users.

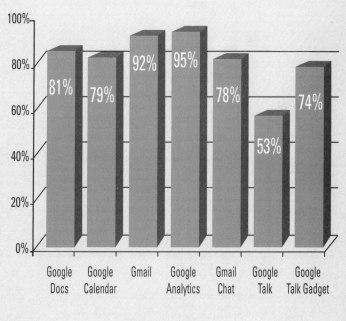

Frequency that Specific Google Applications Were Detected

Spring 2010

Finally, many new business applications also use these same techniques to facilitate ease of operation while minimizing disruptions for customers, partners, and the organization's own security and operations departments. For example, RPC and Sharepoint use port hopping because it is critical to how the protocol or application (respectively) functions, rather than as a means to evade detection or enhance accessibility.

Further emphasizing the fact that many applications are not what they seem to be, the most commonly found applications that can port-hop are a combination of business and personal use applications (see Figure 2-2). Of these, only three are browser-based (Sharepoint, Mediafire, and Ooyla); the others are peer-to-peer or client-server.

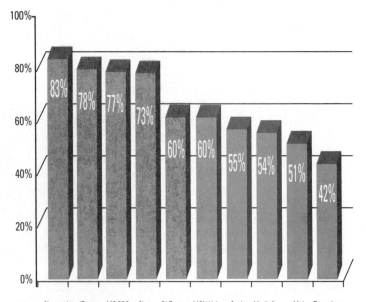

Most Frequently Detected Applications that can Hop Ports

Figure 2-2: Most frequently detected applications that can hop ports.

The result is that HTTP and HTTPS now account for approximately two thirds of all enterprise traffic. This is not a problem, per se, but it does exacerbate an inherent weakness of traditional security infrastructure. Specifically, the wide variety of higher-order applications riding on top of HTTP and HTTPS — whether or not they actually serve a legitimate business purpose — are practically indistinguishable for older network security solutions. The negative impact of organizations further losing control over their network communications is clear and underlines the fact that the application landscape has evolved dramatically.

Threats Are Coming Along for the Ride

The increasing prevalence of application-layer attacks is yet another disturbing trend. Threats that directly target applications can pass right through the majority of enterprise defenses, which have historically been built to provide network-layer protection. Threat developers exploit the same methods (described in the previous section) to infiltrate networks that application developers utilize to promote ease of use and widespread adoption, such as tunneling within applications. The evasion techniques built into these and many other modern applications are being leveraged to provide threats with "free passage" into enterprise networks. It is no surprise, therefore, that greater than 80 percent of all new malware and intrusion attempts are exploiting weaknesses in applications, as opposed to weaknesses in networking components and services. Together with the implicit trust that users place in their applications, all of these factors combine to create a "perfect storm." The motivation for hackers has also shifted — from gaining notoriety to making money. The name of the game today is information theft. Consequently, it is no longer in a hacker's best interests to devise threats that are "noisy" or that are relatively benign. To be successful, a thief must be fast, or stealthy — or both.

For those hackers who favor speed over sophistication — speed of initial threat generation, speed of modification, and speed of propagation — the goal is to develop, launch, and quickly spread new threats immediately on the heels of the disclosure of a new vulnerability. The resulting zero-day and near-zero-day exploits then have an increased likelihood of success because reactive countermeasures, such as patching and those tools that rely on threat signatures (such as antivirus software and intrusion prevention), are unable to keep up — at least during the early phases of a new attack.

This speed-based approach is facilitated in large part by the widespread availability of threat development Web sites, toolkits, and frameworks. Unfortunately, another by-product of these resources is the ability to easily and rapidly convert "known" threats into "unknown" threats — at least from the perspective of signature-based countermeasures. This transformation can be accomplished either by making a minor tweak to the code of a threat, or by adding entirely new propagation and exploit mechanisms, thereby creating what is commonly referred to as a *blended threat.*

Mariposa: How exposed are we?

On July 28, 2010, the U.S. Federal Bureau of Investigation (FBI) announced the arrest of a Slovenian hacker, allegedly the creator of the "Mariposa" botnet — one of the largest criminal botnets ever discovered.

Built with a computer virus known as "Butterfly Bot," the Mariposa botnet steals passwords for Web sites and financial institutions, and is estimated to have infected as many as 8 to 12 million computers in nearly 200 countries. According to Christopher Davis, CEO of Defence Intelligence, it would be easier "to provide a list of the Fortune 1000 companies that *weren't* compromised, rather than the long list of those who were." Financial estimates of the damage to networks and the actual data stolen are still being calculated, and although the bot's creator has been arrested, criminals from around the world who purchased his bot continue to steal data from millions of unsuspecting victims.

Mariposa spreads itself across nine different P2P networks including Ares, BearShare, Direct Connect, eMule, iMesh, Kazaa, Gnutella, BitTorrent (via LimeWire client), and Shareaza. Essentially, for each P2P network, there is a Mariposa foldershare feeding the bot executable. In addition to P2P applications, MSN Instant Messaging is also used as a spreader. The following figure shows the most common Mariposa spreaders found in an analysis of 363 organizations conducted by Palo Alto Networks' Application and Threat Research Team.

Some more detailed analysis of the 363 organizations exposes some sobering statistics:

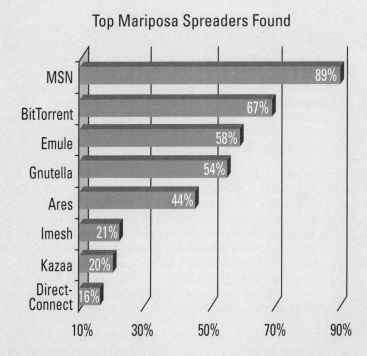

Top Mariposa Spreaders Found

Application	Percent
MSN	89%
BitTorrent	67%
Emule	58%
Gnutella	54%
Ares	44%
Imesh	21%
Kazaa	20%
Direct-Connect	16%

10% 30% 50% 70% 90%

✔ 312 (86 percent) of the organizations had at least one of the P2P applications used by Mariposa.

✔ An average of three of the nine P2P applications were found in each organization.

✔ Total bandwidth consumed by the P2P applications that are capable of spreading Mariposa was 17.3 terabytes or an average of 55 gigabytes per organization.

✔ Session consumption by P2P spreaders was 555 million or an average of 1.8 million sessions per organization.

✔ MSN was found in 322 of the organizations (89 percent).

Resource consumption per organization was 2.8 gigabytes of bandwidth and 67,400 sessions respectively.

With MSN appearing in 89 percent of the organizations and an average of three P2P applications appearing in more than 85 percent of the organizations, it is reasonable to speculate that many organizations are exposed.

The Mariposa botnet is a clear example of how real threats are not just hitching a ride on many of today's most popular applications — they're racking up some serious frequent flyer miles!

Many of today's threats are built to run covertly on networks and systems, quietly collecting sensitive or personal data, and going undetected for as long as possible. This approach helps to preserve the value of the stolen data and enables repeated use of the same exploits and attack vectors. As a result, threats have become increasingly sophisticated. Rootkits, for example, have become more prevalent. These kernel-level exploits effectively mask the presence of other types of malware, enabling them to persistently pursue the nefarious tasks they were designed to accomplish (such as intercepting keystrokes).

Targeted attacks and advanced persistent threats (APTs), such as "Aurora," against specific organizations or individuals are another major concern. In this case, hackers often develop customized attack mechanisms to take advantage of the specific equipment, systems, applications, configurations, and even personnel employed in a specific organization or at a given location, and quietly collect sensitive data over extended periods. According to Verizon's 2010 Data Breach Investigations Report, 70 percent of data breaches resulted from external agents.

The increasing speed and sophistication of threats emphasize the need for proactive countermeasures with extensive visibility and control at the application-layer of the network computing stack.

Chapter 3

Recognizing the Challenges of Legacy Security Infrastructures

A s the application and threat landscape has quickly evolved, the impact within many organizations is that IT has lost control. The inability of their existing security infrastructure to effectively distinguish good or desirable applications from those that are bad or unwanted, forces most IT shops to take an inflexible and untenable "all-or-nothing" approach to security, in which they either/or:

✔ Take a permissive stance — an approach that ensures the accessibility of important applications, but also allows unwanted applications and threats on the corporate network

✔ Just say "no" in order to maintain a high state of security, but at the risk of limiting business agility and productivity, alienating users and business units, and creating an underground subculture of backdoor processes to circumvent security controls.

Instead, IT needs the capability to exert granular control and provide in-depth protection down to the level of individual applications, in order to confidently say "yes" to legitimate requests from the business and its end-users. Unfortunately, traditional network security infrastructures have failed to keep pace and are unable to provide this functionality.

In this chapter, you find out how the new application and threat landscape has challenged these legacy security devices, particularly firewalls, beyond their capability to effectively protect today's networks.

Whatever Happened to the Firewall?

Have you noticed that nobody gets excited about a firewall anymore? There was a time when the firewall was the single most important security device in your network. So what happened?

The answer is a bit of a cliché, but — the Internet has changed everything! Years ago, most firewalls did a pretty good job of controlling traffic in and out of corporate networks. That's because application traffic was generally well behaved. E-mail would typically flow through port 25, FTP was assigned to port 20, and the whole "Web surfing" was hanging, uhhh, port 80. Everybody played by the rules that "ports + protocols = applications" and the firewall had everything under control. Blocking a port meant blocking an application. Nice and simple.

Unfortunately, the Internet has never really been nice and simple. And that is truer today than ever before. Today, the Internet often accounts for 70 percent or more of the traffic on your corporate network. And it's not just port 80 Web surfing. Typically, 20 to 30 percent of it is encrypted SSL traffic on port 443. Even worse, there is a plethora of new Internet applications that insist on making their own rules. They wrap themselves in other protocols, sneak through ports that don't belong to them, and bury themselves inside SSL tunnels. In short, they just don't play fair.

All these applications carry some inherent risk to your business. And they play host to clever new threats that can slip through your firewall undetected. Meanwhile, your firewall just sits there like nothing is wrong because it's still playing by rules that don't exist anymore!

Port-based firewalls have poor vision

Because they are deployed in-line at critical network junctions, firewalls see all traffic and, therefore, are the ideal resource to provide granular access control. The problem, however, is that most firewalls are "far-sighted." They can see the general shape of things, but not the finer details of what is actually happening. This is because they operate by inferring the application-layer service that a given stream of traffic is associated with, based on the port number used in the packet's header, and they only look at the first packet in a session to determine the type of traffic being processed, typically to improve performance. They rely on a convention — not a requirement — that a given port corresponds to a given service (for example, TCP port 80 corresponds to HTTP). As such, they are also incapable of distinguishing between different applications that use the same port/service (see Figure 3-1).

Figure 3-1: Port-based firewalls can't see or control applications

The net result is that traditional, "port-based" firewalls have basically gone blind. Besides being unable to account for common evasion techniques such as port hopping, protocol tunneling, and the use of nonstandard ports, these firewalls simply lack the visibility and intelligence to discern which network traffic

- Corresponds to applications that serve a legitimate business purpose

- Corresponds to applications that can serve a legitimate business purpose but, in a given instance, are being used for unsanctioned activities

- Should be blocked because it includes malware or other types of threats, even though it corresponds to legitimate business activities

On top of everything else, their control model is typically too coarse-grained. Said firewalls can either block or allow traffic, but offer little variation in between to craft a more appropriate response for all of the "gray" applications that enterprises would ultimately like to support — for example, by allowing certain functions within an application but not others, allowing but also applying traffic-shaping policies, allowing but scanning for threats or confidential data, or allowing based on users, groups, or time of day.

It doesn't really help matters that the most common steps taken to address the inadequacies of traditional firewalls have, for all intents and purposes, been completely unsuccessful.

Bolt-on functionality is fundamentally flawed

Many purveyors of traditional firewalls have attempted to correct the far-sighted nature of their products by incorporating deep packet inspection (DPI) capabilities. On the surface, adding a measure of application-layer visibility and control in this manner appears to be a reasonable approach. However, the boost in security effectiveness that can be achieved in most cases is only incremental because the additional capability is being "bolted on," and the foundation it is being bolted on to is weak to begin with. In other words, the new functionality is added on rather than integrated, and the port-based firewall, with its complete lack of application awareness, is still used for initial classification of all traffic. The problems and limitations this leads to include

- **Applications that should not be on the network are allowed onto the network.**

- **Not everything that should be inspected necessarily gets inspected.** Because the firewall is unable to accurately classify application traffic, deciding which sessions to pass along to the DPI engine becomes a hit-or-miss proposition.

- **Policy management gets convoluted.** Rules on how to handle individual applications essentially get "nested" within the DPI portion of the product — which itself is engaged as part of a higher/outer level access control policy.

- **Inadequate performance forces compromises to be made.** Inefficient use of system resources and CPU and memory intensive application-layer functionality put considerable strain on the underlying platform. To account for this situation, administrators can only implement advanced filtering capabilities selectively.

Firewall "helpers" don't help

Over the years, enterprises have also tried to compensate for their firewalls' deficiencies by implementing a range of supplementary security solutions, often in the form of standalone appliances. Intrusion prevention systems, antivirus gateways, Web filtering products, and application-specific solutions — such as a dedicated platform for instant messaging security — are just a handful of the more popular choices. Unfortunately, the outcome is disappointingly similar to that of the DPI approach, with an additional twist.

Not everything that should get inspected does because these firewall helpers either can't see all of the traffic, rely on the same port- and protocol-based classification scheme that has failed the legacy firewall, or only provide coverage for a limited set of applications. Policy management is an even greater problem given that access control rules and inspection requirements are spread among several consoles and involve multiple policy models. And performance is still an issue as well, at least in terms of having a relatively high aggregate latency.

Then comes the kicker: device sprawl. As one "solution" after another is added to the network, the device count, degree of complexity, and total cost of ownership all continue to rise. Capital costs for the products themselves and all of the supporting infrastructure that is required are joined by a substantial collection of recurring operational expenditures, including support/maintenance contracts, content subscriptions, and facilities costs (power, cooling, and floor space) — not to mention an array of "soft" costs such as those pertaining to IT productivity, training, and vendor management. The result is an unwieldy, ineffective, and costly endeavor that is simply not sustainable.

Traditional IPS Is a Poor Match for Today's Threats

Intrusion Prevention Systems (IPS) detect and block attacks focused on vulnerabilities that exist in systems and applications. Unlike Intrusion Detection Systems (IDS) that focus only on alerting, IPS systems are intended to be deployed in-line to actively block attacks as they are detected. One of the core capabilities of an IPS is the ability to decode protocols to more accurately apply signatures. This allows IPS signatures to be applied to very specific portions of traffic, thereby reducing the percentage of false positives that were often experienced with signature-only systems. It is important to note that most IPS offerings will use port and protocol as the first pass of traffic classification, which, given the evasive characteristics of today's applications, may lead to an erroneous identification of the application. And because IPS systems are focused mainly on attacks, they are typically deployed in conjunction with a firewall as a separate appliance or as a combination firewall and IPS.

IPS is designed to stop threats using a "find it and kill it" approach. It is not designed to control applications. But even for stopping threats, IPS has its flaws.

Given the new application and threat landscape, organizations are also reexamining traditional intrusion prevention systems (IPS). The major IPS vendors are struggling to differentiate across several basic elements of IPS:

> ✔ **Server and data center protection.** There are only a handful of detection and prevention techniques, and

most IPS products support them all. These techniques include protocol anomaly detection, stateful pattern matching, statistical anomaly detection, heuristic analysis, blocking of invalid or malformed packets, and IP defragmentation and TCP reassembly (for anti-evasion). Most IPS vendors also use vulnerability-facing signatures (as opposed to exploit-facing signatures) and turn off server-to-client protection to improve performance.

✔ **Research and support.** This comes down to how much actual research vendors are doing, and how quickly they can respond to help enterprises protect against new attacks and vulnerabilities. Much is made of the efforts of the research teams of IPS vendors, and while there certainly are differences, much of the research is outsourced to a few industry research stalwarts. The other aspect is critical — regardless of who does the research — can the vendor deliver timely updates to protect customers from new and emerging threats?

✔ **Performance.** Organizations are clearly sensitized to IPS performance issues. A recent *Infonetics* study cited the introduction of traffic/application latency and bandwidth/performance as major concerns causing enterprises to deploy "out-of-band" IPS. Clearly, being able to keep up with enterprise expectations for throughput and latency is top of mind for many customers.

As defenses mature, however, attackers evolve. Given that intrusion detection and prevention systems, like firewalls, are based on legacy techniques that are relatively well-understood, new attacks are able to exploit well-known weak spots, including

✔ **Application-borne threats.** Threat developers are using applications, both as targets and as transmission vectors. Applications provide fertile ground for both methods. Some application-borne threats are well understood (for example, many of the threats that move across social networks — Koobface, Boface, or Fbaction) — others are not (such as Mariposa, using MSN Messenger and P2P file sharing applications to spread). Regardless, attackers find it far easier to piggyback on applications, and start their attack with the client.

✔ **Encrypted threat vectors.** The other important technique that threats employ is encryption. While security researchers have warned for years that encryption can be used by various threats, encrypted attacks still need a conduit — enter user-centric applications. Users are easily duped into clicking on encrypted links (too many users think that HTTPS means "safe"), which can send encrypted threats sailing through enterprise defenses. This is increasingly simple on social networks, where the level of trust is extremely high. The other closely related vector is obfuscation via compression — traditional IPS can't decompress, and thus can't scan compressed content.

A common theme here is the level of control needed to prevent these newer threats — controlling applications and content, decrypting SSL, unzipping content to look for threats — all of which goes well beyond what IPS traditionally does. A major limitation of IPS, despite all of the work to transition from IDS (intrusion detection systems), is that it remains a negative security model, and is architected as such. Put more simply, IPS relies on a "find it and kill it" model — which doesn't work very well for the types of control necessary to deal with many of these new threats that move over applications. Nor does it lend itself to an architecture and platform capable of decrypting and classifying all traffic.

A positive security model operates by expressly allowing all communications that are known to be benign, appropriate, or necessary, and excluding everything else. A negative security model operates by seeking to classify only undesirable communications and content, and employing countermeasures for those that are known to be bad.

A word on data leaks

Some of the biggest information-security news stories over the past two years involve the leaking of confidential or sensitive organizational data via applications (for example, U.S. government agencies and contractors, pharmaceuticals, and retailers). In most cases, the applications that the data leaked across were expressly forbidden — unfortunately, their policies couldn't be enforced with traditional firewalls and IPS. Given these high-profile security breaches, it is no wonder that organizations are starting to look for a better solution to help protect against such embarrassing incidents.

UTM Only Makes What Is Broken Cheaper

Unified Threat Management (UTM) devices are another new approach to modern security challenges that are based on traditional techniques. UTM solutions were born as security vendors began bolting intrusion prevention and antivirus add-ons to their stateful firewalls in an effort to reduce the cost of deployment. UTM products do not perform their functions any better than stand-alone devices. Instead, they provide convenience to the customer by integrating multiple functions into one device. Unfortunately, UTMs have a reputation for being inaccurate, hard to manage, and performing poorly when services are enabled, relegating them to environments where the value of device consolidation outweighs the downside of lost functionality, manageability, or performance.

The primary advantage of the UTM solution is that it typically does a reasonable job of addressing the issues associated with device sprawl. Instead of having all of the "helper" countermeasures deployed as separate devices, with UTM they all come in one physical package.

But so what? The result is really no different than the bolted-on approach and, therefore, exhibits the same deficiencies. Inadequate application classification and resulting blind spots in the inspections that are performed remain as fundamental problems, while performance and policy management issues are compounded even further based on having to account for multiple additional countermeasures instead of just one.

It's Time to Fix the Firewall

Traditional port-based firewalls really don't provide any value anymore — not in a world where network boundaries are disintegrating and Internet applications are exploding.

But you already know that, which is why you've been forced to make up for their glaring deficiencies with more specialized appliances — intrusion prevention systems, proxies, antivirus, anti-spyware, URL filtering, and more. Sure, these tools add some incremental value, but it's getting harder to justify their additional cost and complexity — especially during challenging economic times.

More security appliances don't necessarily mean a more secure environment. In fact, the complexity and inconsistency associated with such an approach can actually be a detriment to your organization's security.

In a February 2009 interview with *Network World* magazine, Craig Shumard, Chief Information Security Officer (CISO) at Cigna, referred to the growing stack of security products in his organization as "unsustainable" and likened it to the "leaning tower of Pisa," saying "we can't continue to operate 15 to 25, or more, security products . . . we [can't] continue to just add new security products to the environment and expect that we will use them effectively." Clearly, it's a strategy that does not scale. More importantly, none of these additional products give you the visibility and control you need over the applications running on your network.

It's time to address the core problem. It's time to fix the firewall! After all, the firewall sits at the most critically important place in the network, and really should be that centralized point of visibility and control over everything entering and leaving the network.

Chapter 4

Solving the Problem with Next-Generation Firewalls

*N*etwork security in most enterprises is fragmented and broken, exposing them to unwanted business risks and ever-rising costs. Traditional network security solutions have failed to keep pace with changes to applications, threats, and the networking landscape. Furthermore, the remedies put forth to compensate for their deficiencies have, for the most part, proven ineffective. It is time to reinvent network security.

This chapter is about next-generation firewalls (NGFWs): what a next-generation firewall is, what it isn't, and how it can benefit your organization.

The Next-Generation Firewall

To restore the firewall as the cornerstone of enterprise network security, next-generation firewalls "fix the problem at its core." Starting with a blank slate, next-generation firewalls classify traffic by the application's identity in order to enable visibility and control of all types of applications — including Web 2.0, Enterprise 2.0, and legacy — running on enterprise networks. The essential functional requirements for an effective next-generation firewall include the ability to:

- ✔ Identify applications regardless of port, protocol, evasive techniques, or SSL encryption before doing anything else

- ✔ Provide visibility of and granular, policy-based control over applications, including individual functions

- ✔ Accurately identify users and subsequently use identity information as an attribute for policy control

- ✔ Provide real-time protection against a wide array of threats, including those operating at the application layer

- ✔ Integrate, not just combine, traditional firewall and network intrusion prevention capabilities

- ✔ Support multi-gigabit, in-line deployments with negligible performance degradation

Typical capabilities of traditional firewalls include packet filtering, network- and port-address translation (NAT), stateful inspection, and virtual private network (VPN) support. Typical intrusion prevention capabilities include vulnerability- and threat-facing signatures, and heuristics.

The key to NGFWs is the ability to do everything a traditional firewall does with the advanced capabilities that combine innovative identification technologies, high-performance, and additional foundational features to yield an enterprise-class solution.

Application identification

Establishing port and protocol is an important first step in application identification but, by itself, is insufficient. Robust application identification and inspection enables granular control of the flow of sessions through a firewall based on the specific applications that are being used, instead of just relying on the underlying set of often indistinguishable network communication services (see Figure 4-1).

Positive application identification is the traffic classification engine at the heart of NGFWs. It requires a multi-factor approach to determine the identity of applications on the network, regardless of port, protocol, encryption, or evasive tactics. Application identification techniques used in NGFWs (see Figure 4-2) include

✔ **Application protocol detection and decryption.** Determines the application protocol (for example, HTTP) and, if SSL is in use, decrypts the traffic so that it can be analyzed further. Traffic is reencrypted after all the identification technologies have had an opportunity to operate.

✔ **Application protocol decoding.** Determines whether the initially detected application protocol is the "real one," or if it is being used as a tunnel to hide the actual application (for example, Yahoo! Instant Messenger might be inside HTTP).

✔ **Application signatures.** Context-based signatures look for unique properties and transaction characteristics to correctly identify the application regardless of the port and protocol being used. This includes the ability to detect specific functions within applications (such as file transfers within IM sessions).

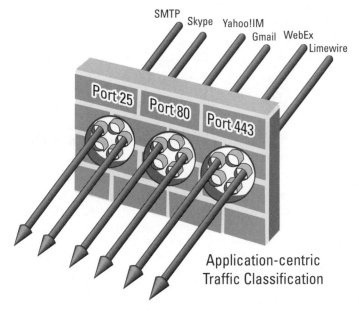

Figure 4-1: Application-centric traffic classification identifies specific applications flowing across the network, irrespective of the port and protocol in use.

✔ **Heuristics.** For traffic that eludes identification by signature analysis, heuristic (or behavioral) analyses are
applied — enabling identification of any troublesome
applications, such as P2P or VoIP tools that use proprietary encryption.

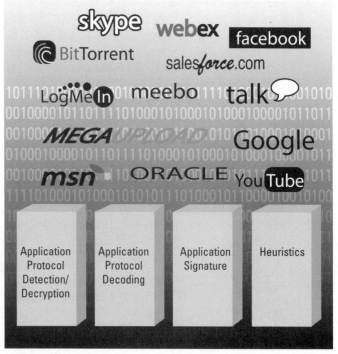

Figure 4-2: NGFW techniques used to identify applications regardless of
port, protocol, evasive tactic, or SSL encryption.

Having the technology to accurately identify applications is
important, but understanding the security implications of an
application so that an informed policy decision can be made
is equally important. Look for a NGFW solution that includes
information about each application, and its behaviors and
risks, to provide IT administrators with application knowledge
such as known vulnerabilities, ability to evade detection, file
transfer capabilities, bandwidth consumption, malware transmission, and potential for misuse.

User identification

User identification technology links IP addresses to specific user identities, enabling visibility and control of network activity on a per-user basis. Tight integration with LDAP directories, such as Microsoft Active Directory (AD), supports this objective in two ways. First, it regularly verifies and maintains the user-to-IP address relationship using a combination of login monitoring, end-station polling, and captive portal techniques. Next, it communicates with AD to harvest relevant user information, such as role and group assignments. These details are then available to:

 ✔ Gain visibility into who specifically is responsible for all application, content, and threat traffic on the network

 ✔ Enable the use of identity as a variable within access control policies

 ✔ Facilitate troubleshooting/incident response and reportings

With user identification, IT departments get another powerful mechanism to help control the use of applications in an intelligent manner. For example, a social networking application that would otherwise be blocked because of its risky nature can be enabled for individuals or groups that have a legitimate need to use it, such as the human resources department (see Figure 4-3).

Content identification

Content identification infuses next-generation firewalls with capabilities previously unheard of in enterprise firewalls, such as real-time prevention of threats within permitted traffic, control of Web surfing activities, and file and data filtering.

 ✔ **Threat prevention.** This component prevents spyware, viruses, and vulnerabilities from penetrating the network, regardless of the application traffic on which they ride.

   • **Application decoder.** Pre-processes data streams and inspects it for specific threat identifiers.

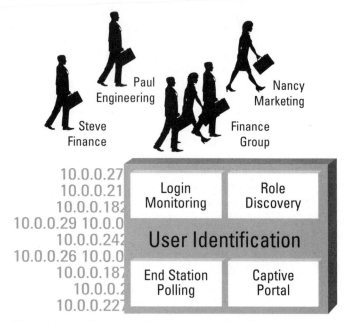

Figure 4-3: User identification integrates enterprise directories for user-based policies, reporting, and forensics.

- **Stream-based virus and spyware scanning.** Scanning traffic as soon as the first packets of a file are received — as opposed to waiting until the entire file is in memory — maximizes throughput and minimizes latency.

- **Uniform threat signature format.** Performance is enhanced by avoiding the need to use separate scanning engines for each type of threat. Viruses, spyware, and vulnerability exploits can all be detected in a single pass.

- **Vulnerability attack protection (IPS).** Robust routines for traffic normalization and defragmentation are joined by protocol-anomaly, behavior-anomaly, and heuristic detection mechanisms to provide protection from the widest range of both known and unknown threats.

✔ **URL filtering.** Although not required, URL filtering is another tool sometimes used to classify content. An integrated, on-box URL database allows administrators to monitor and control Web surfing activities of employees and guest users. Employed in conjunction with user identification, Web usage policies can even be set on a per-user basis, further safeguarding the enterprise from an array of legal, regulatory, and productivity related risks.

✔ **File and data filtering.** Taking advantage of in-depth application inspection, file and data filtering enables enforcement of policies that reduce the risk of unauthorized file and data transfer. Capabilities include the ability to block files by their actual type (not based on just their extension), and the ability to control the transfer of sensitive data patterns such as credit card numbers. This complements the granularity of application identification, which for many applications offers the ability to control file transfer within an individual application (such as IM).

With content identification, IT departments gain the ability to stop threats, reduce inappropriate use of the Internet, and help prevent data leaks — all without having to invest in a pile of additional products and risk appliance sprawl (see Figure 4-4).

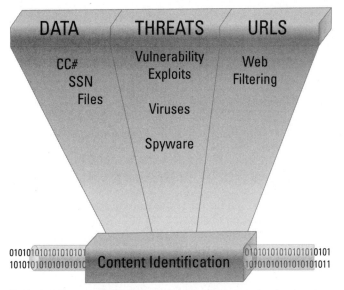

Figure 4-4: Content identification unifies content scanning for threats, confidential data, and URL filtering.

Policy control

Identifying the applications in use (application identification), who is using them (user identification), and what they are using them for (content identification) is an important first step in learning about the traffic traversing the network. Learning what the application does, the ports it uses, its underlying technology, and its behavior is the next step towards making an informed decision about how to treat the application. Once a complete picture of usage is gained, organizations can apply policies with a range of responses that are more fine-grained and appropriate than simply "allow" or "deny" — the only options available in traditional port-based firewalls. This is made possible by the combination of application-, user-, and content identification, and the positive security model of next-generation firewalls. Traditional port-based firewalls have the security model, but lack intelligence. Other security devices might have some of the intelligence, but not the security model. Examples of policy control options in NGFWs include

- Allow or deny
- Allow but scan for exploits, viruses, and other threats
- Allow based on schedule, users, or groups
- Decrypt and inspect
- Apply traffic shaping through QoS
- Apply policy-based forwarding
- Allow certain application functions
- Any combination of the aforementioned

High-performance architecture

Having a comprehensive suite of application awareness and content inspection capabilities is of little value if IT administrators are unable to fully engage them due to performance constraints. Therefore, it is important to select a next-generation firewall that is designed from the start to deliver high performance. The issue is not just that these capabilities are inherently resource intensive. There's also the tremendous traffic volume confronting today's security infrastructure, not to mention the latency sensitivity of many applications. Rated throughput and reasonable latency should be sustainable under heavy loads, even when all application and threat inspection features are engaged simultaneously — which is the ideal configuration from a security perspective.

For traditional security products, especially those with bolted-on capabilities, each high-level security function is performed independently. This multi-pass approach requires low-level packet processing routines to be repeated numerous times. System resources are used inefficiently and significant latency is introduced (see Figure 4-5).

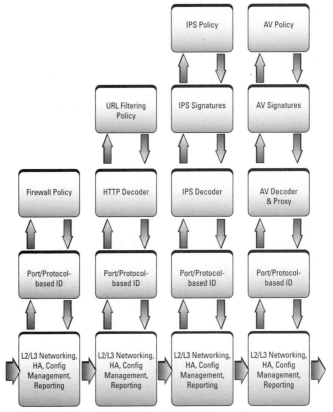

Figure 4-5: Legacy multi-pass architectures.

In contrast, a NGFW that uses a single-pass architecture eliminates repetitive handling of packets, reducing the burden placed on hardware and minimizing latency. Other innovations, such as customized hardware architecture that maintains separate data and control planes, help provide an enterprise-class solution (see Figure 4-6).

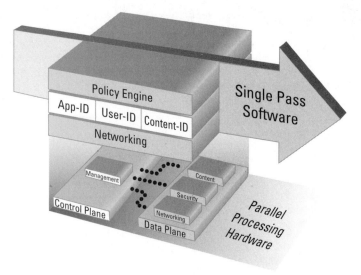

Figure 4-6: Single-pass parallel processing architecture and separate control and data planes provide enterprise performance.

What a Next-Generation Firewall Isn't

There are many network-based security products available that perform functions similar to a next-generation firewall, but they are not the same thing. Examples include

- ✔ **Unified threat management (UTM).** UTM appliances host multiple security functions, such as port-based firewall capabilities and basic intrusion prevention. UTM solutions are not typically built for high performance and are typically adequate only in smaller environments.

✔ **Proxy-based products.** Proxies (both firewall and caching) sit between source and destination, intercepting traffic and inspecting it by terminating the application session and reinitiating it to the target destination. The proxy establishes the connection with the destination, on behalf of the client, hiding computers on the network behind the proxy. However, only a limited number of applications can be supported because each individual application has to have its own proxy.

✔ **Web application firewalls (WAFs).** A WAF is designed to look at Web applications, monitoring them for security issues that may arise due to possible coding errors. WAFs look only at Layer 7, rather than inspecting the entire OSI stack.

WAFs protect applications, and NGFWs protect networks.

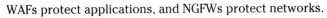

✔ **Vulnerability and patch management.** Vulnerability and patch management solutions scan hosts for known vulnerabilities in software and operating systems, verify that patches and updates are installed, and correct the identified vulnerability. This is not a function of NGFWs.

✔ **Data loss prevention (DLP).** These solutions prevent transmission of data that matches an identified pattern (such as credit card numbers). These solutions are implemented for network functions with no real-time requirements regarding speed and latency.

✔ **Secure Web gateways.** These solutions use URL categorization to enforce policies regarding user access to Web sites and block malware propagated by malicious Web sites. Compared to NGFWs, these solutions have limited capabilities and are easily circumvented by users.

✔ **Secure messaging gateways.** These include spam filters and IM gateways, and provide anti-spam and anti-phishing protection, antivirus scanning, attachment filtering, content filtering, data loss prevention, and policy compliance and reporting. Unlike NGFWs, these functions are not performed in real-time and are used for applications like e-mail, which is less latency sensitive.

Benefits of Next-Generation Firewalls

Next-generation firewalls produce numerous benefits over traditional network security infrastructures and solutions. These include

- **Visibility and control.** The enhanced visibility and control provided by NGFWs enable enterprises to focus on business relevant elements such as applications, users, and content for policy controls, instead of having to rely on nebulous and misleading attributes like ports and protocols, and to better and more thoroughly manage risks and achieve compliance, while providing threat prevention for allowed applications.

- **Safe enablement.** Achieve comprehensive coverage — by providing a consistent set of protection and enablement capabilities for all users, regardless of their location.

- **Simplification.** Reduce complexity of the network security and its administration — by obviating the need for numerous stand-alone products. This consolidation reduces hard capital costs, as well as ongoing "hard" operational expenses, such as support, maintenance, and software subscriptions, power and HVAC, and "soft" operational expenses, such as training and management.

- **IT and business alignment.** Enable IT to confidently say "yes" to the applications needed to best support the business — by giving them the ability to identify and granularly control applications while protecting against a broad array of threats.

Chapter 5

Deploying Next-Generation Firewalls

- -

In This Chapter

▶ Implementing employee, desktop, and network controls

▶ Asking the right questions to help you choose the best solution

▶ Designing your network for optimum performance and security

- -

*F*ar too often, technical solutions are implemented without considering the implications for an organization's overall security strategy. To avoid this mistake, it is important to ensure that your policies are up to date and the technology solutions you are considering support a comprehensive security strategy.

When considering various technology solutions, it is also important to have a clear understanding of your organization's requirements. According to Gartner, there are fewer points of differentiation in the enterprise firewall market, and therefore organizations must drive their final product selection decisions by their specific requirements.

This chapter describes the different types of controls that must be considered in an organization's security policies and provides specific examples of technical requirements you need to explore as you define your requirements and develop a Request For Proposal (RFP) for your vendors. Finally, it covers the importance of properly segmenting your network and sensitive data, and how to address mobile users.

Safe Enablement through Smart Policies

Enablement is first and foremost about education and knowledge of applications, behavior, risks, and users. In the case of Enterprise 2.0 applications, the users have long since decided on the benefits, although there continue to be opportunities for education on the choice of the best application for the job. IT's role is that of an advisor and mentor, advising users about risks and behaviors — and guiding them regarding which of the array of available applications might be best at solving their requirements. But enablement is also about raising the awareness of the risks associated with applications. For that, IT workers need to become true super-users themselves, albeit in a different sense of that term than usual. An Enterprise 2.0 super-user is someone who "lives" inside the application and relies on it for a major set of tasks. For IT to be relevant, it needs to adopt Enterprise 2.0 wholeheartedly and without prejudice. Once that's achieved, IT can successfully educate the users on all the risks associated with the use of Enterprise 2.0 applications — even those that pertain to the social and reputational implications of their use.

For governance to be effective, IT needs to take a major role in the definition of smart policies. But it is critical for IT not to be the sole owner of these policies, as their effectiveness and relevance are inversely proportional to the amount of classic IT thinking. This may sound highly controversial, but Enterprise 2.0 applications have a tendency to become the "forbidden fruit." And while most Enterprise 2.0 adoption starts from the bottom up, it won't go very far without executive sponsorship and support. This implies that while IT may try to stop the use of Enterprise 2.0 applications, once they've been successfully adopted, IT can no longer count on executive support to do that.

Often times the governance discussion is illustrated with examples of mistakes that users made while using certain types of Enterprise 2.0 applications, such as social media. It's an easy argument for IT, but it's ultimately a losing one. Nor is it a smart idea for IT to pursue a compliance-based argument for the simple reason that no legislation exists, per se, that governs the use of Enterprise 2.0 applications. It comes down to using the right tool for the job and being smart about it. For example, in a heavily regulated environment such as stock trading, the use of instant messaging may be prone to retention and auditability rules. IT's role is to educate the traders on the implications of each of the tools, participate in the development of the use policy, and subsequently monitor and enforce its use. In this example, that policy could prevent the traders from using Facebook chat for instant messaging, but enable MSN for that use instead.

 Governance and its management counterpart work best if they're based on a set of smart corporate policies that are developed by the four major stakeholders in the Enterprise 2.0 landscape; IT, HR, executive management, and the users. Clearly IT has a role to play, but it can't be the strictly defined role that it so often plays, nor can it be lax about its role as the enabler and governor of applications and technology.

 If application controls are going to be implemented and enforced, they should be part of the overarching corporate security policy. As part of the process of implementing an application control policy, IT should make a concerted effort to learn about Enterprise 2.0 applications. This includes embracing them for all their intended purposes and, if needed, proactively installing them or enabling them in a lab environment to see how they act. Peer discussions, Enterprise 2.0-focused Web sites, message boards, blogs, and developer communities are valuable sources of information.

Employee controls

Most companies have some type of application usage policy, outlining which applications are allowed and which are prohibited. Every employee is expected to understand the contents of this policy and the ramifications of not complying with it, but there are a number of unanswered questions, including

- Given the increasing number of "bad" applications, how will an employee know which applications are allowed and which are prohibited?
- How is the list of unapproved applications updated, and who ensures employees know the list has changed?
- What constitutes a policy violation?
- What are the ramifications of policy violations — firing or a reprimand?

The development of policy guidelines is often challenging as tension between risk and reward has polarized opinions about what should be allowed and what should be prohibited. At the core of the issue is the fact that the two organizational groups that are typically involved in policy development — IT security and HR — have largely been sidelined during adoption of new technologies. To build a policy for safe use after new technologies and applications have been implemented is no easy task.

Documented employee policies need to be a key piece of the application control puzzle, but employee controls as a stand-alone mechanism will remain largely ineffective for safe enablement of Enterprise 2.0 applications.

Desktop controls

Desktop controls present IT departments with significant challenges. Careful consideration should be applied to the granularity of the desktop controls and the impact on employee productivity. As with employee policies, desktop controls are a key piece to the safe enablement of Enterprise 2.0 applications in the enterprise, and if used alone, will be ineffective for several reasons.

The drastic step of desktop lockdown to keep users from installing their own applications is a task that is easier said than done.

- ✔ Laptops connecting remotely, Internet downloads, USB drives, and e-mail are all means of installing applications that may or may not be approved.

- ✔ Removing administrative rights completely has proven to be difficult to implement and, in some cases, limits end-user capabilities.

- ✔ USB drives are now capable of running applications, so an Enterprise 2.0 application can, in effect, be accessed after the network admission is granted.

Desktop controls can complement the documented employee policies as a means to safely enable Enterprise 2.0 applications.

Network controls

At the network level, what is needed is a means to identify Enterprise 2.0 applications and block or control them. By implementing network level controls, IT is able to minimize the possibility of threats and disruptions stemming from the use of Enterprise 2.0 applications. Several possible control mechanisms can be used at the network level, each of which carries certain drawbacks that reduce their effectiveness.

✔ Stateful firewalls can be used as a first line of defense, providing coarse filtering of traffic and segmenting the network into different password-protected zones. One drawback to stateful firewalls is that they use protocol and port to identify and control what gets in and out of the network. This port-centric design is relatively ineffective when faced with Enterprise 2.0 applications that hop from port to port until they find an open connection to the network.

✔ IPS added to a firewall deployment enhances the network threat-prevention capability by looking at a subset of traffic and blocking known threats or bad applications. IPS offerings lack the breadth of applications and the performance required to look at all traffic across all ports and as such, cannot be considered a full solution.

✔ IPS technologies are typically designed to look only at a partial set of traffic to avoid impeding performance and, as such, would be unable to cover the breadth of applications needed by today's enterprises. And finally, managing a firewall and IPS combination is usually a cumbersome task, requiring different management interfaces pointed at separate policy tables. Simply put, the current bolt-on solutions do not have the accuracy, policy, or performance to solve today's application visibility and control requirements.

✔ Proxy solutions are another means of traffic control but here too, they look at a limited set of applications or protocols and as such only see a partial set of the traffic that needs to be monitored. So an Enterprise 2.0 application will merely see a port blocked by a proxy and hop over to the next one that is open. By design, proxies need to mimic the application they are trying to control so they struggle with updates to existing applications as well as development of proxies for new applications. A final issue that plagues proxy solutions is throughput performance brought on by how the proxy terminates the application, and then forwards it on to its destination.

The challenge with any of these network controls is that they do not have the ability to identify Enterprise 2.0 applications; they look at only a portion of the traffic and suffer from performance issues.

Defining Your Requirements and Developing an RFP

After creating or updating your organization's security policies, it's time to define your organization's requirements for a next-generation firewall solution. At a very high level, this includes doing your due diligence on the vendors you are considering. You should be asking questions about your potential vendors, such as:

- ✔ What is the company's vision and how well does it execute on that vision?

- ✔ How innovative is the company?

- ✔ What is the company's culture?

- ✔ What is its development process? What is its quality assurance process?

- ✔ What is the size and financial condition of the company?

- ✔ Is the company a potential acquisition target? If so, is it more likely to be acquired in order to quickly gain an edge because of its innovation and proprietary technology, or to kill off a competitor?

- ✔ How large is its installed customer base?

- ✔ Does it have other customers (perhaps even competitors) that are in a similar industry as your own organization?

- ✔ Does it have any reference accounts or customer success stories to share?

Next, define your organization's technical requirements. Fortunately, you don't necessarily have to reinvent the wheel here. Begin by taking a look at your organization's security policies (see the previous section) to see what capabilities will be needed in order to implement and support those policies.

There are also plenty of examples of firewall and network security requirements practically everywhere. In fact, most regulatory compliance requirements relating to data protection are based on information security best practices. Even if your organization isn't subject to any of these regulations, using them for guidance isn't necessarily a bad thing. For example, the Payment Card Industry Data Security Standard (PCI DSS), which is applicable to *every* organization that processes a credit or debit card, defines several firewall requirements, all of which can easily be modified and incorporated into a formal RFP for your organization.

Drilling down into specific feature requirements, your RFP should address several requirements, including application identification, application policy control, threat prevention, management, networking, and hardware.

- ✔ **Application identification.** Describe how the gateway will accurately identify applications and the mechanisms used to classify applications.

    - Is identification based on IPS or DPI technology? If so, how are accuracy, completeness, and performance issues addressed when scanning network traffic?

    - How is the traffic classification mechanism differentiated from other vendors?

    - How are unknown applications handled?

    - Are custom application signatures supported?

    - How is SSL-encrypted traffic identified, inspected, and controlled?

    - How do the SSL controls delineate between personal (such as banking, shopping, and health) and nonpersonal traffic?

    - How many applications are identified (provide a list) and what is the process for updating the application database (for example, software upgrade or dynamic update)?

- If a new application is needed, what is the process for adding it to the device?

- Can an end-user submit an application for identification and analysis and/or define custom applications?

- Does the product support URL filtering? Describe the URL filtering database. Is the database located on the device or on another device?

- Describe/list any other security functions that can leverage the application information collected, including drilldown details and user visibility features.

✔ **Application policy control.** Describe the process for implementing policy-based application controls, all application policy control parameters (such as user, IP address, date/time), and how they can be used.

- Can policy controls be implemented for all applications identified?

- Can policy controls be implemented for specific users or groups?

- How are remote access environments supported (for example, Citrix and Terminal Services)?

- Can port-based controls be implemented for all applications in the application database?

- Can the solution perform traditional firewall-based access controls?

- Can policy controls be implemented from a single management interface?

- Are users warned when they attempt to access a URL or application that violates policy?

✔ **Threat prevention.** Describe the intrusion prevention features and antivirus engine.

- List the types of threats that can be blocked. List the file types that can be blocked.

- Is data filtering supported?

- Can the threat prevention engine scan inside SSL-encrypted traffic? Compressed traffic?

✔ **Management.** Describe the management capabilities and visibility tools that enable a clear picture of the traffic on the network.

- Does device management require a separate server or device?

- Are application policy controls, firewall policy controls, and threat prevention features all enabled from the same policy editor?

- What tools provide a summary view of the applications, threats, and URLs on the network?

- Describe any log visualization tools.

- Are reporting tools available to understand how the network is being used and to highlight changes in network usage?

- Describe the logging and reporting capabilities of the solution.

- Describe how management access is ensured when the device is under heavy traffic load.

- Are there any central management tools available?

✔ **Networking.** Describe the network integration and implementation capabilities.

- Describe any Layer 2 or Layer 3 capabilities.

- Are 802.1q VLANs supported? What is the VLAN capacity?

- Is dynamic routing supported (for example, OSPF, BGP, and RIP)?

- Describe any QoS or traffic shaping features.

- Is IPv6 supported?

- Are IPSec VPNs supported? SSL VPNs?

- What deployment options are available (for example, in-line, tap, passive)?

- Describe any high availability (HA) capabilities.

✔ **Hardware.** Is the solution software-based, an OEM server, or a purpose-built appliance? Describe the architecture.

Deployment Flexibility Matters

It's important to design your network to maximize performance and efficiency. Properly deploying a NGFW in the most optimal location or locations on your network is no less important. Segmentation is a key concept in the proper design of networks and deployment of firewalls. While there are many different ways to segment a network, next-generation firewalls bring a unique combination of hardware- and software-related segmentation capabilities that enable organizations to isolate key sections of their network, such as a datacenter.

The concept of security zones, which for purposes of isolating sensitive data or critical network infrastructure (again, for example, a datacenter), are roughly equivalent to network segments (see Figure 5-1). A security zone is a logical container for physical interfaces, VLANs, a range of IP addresses, or a combination thereof. Interfaces that are added to each security zone can be configured in Layer 2, Layer 3, or a mixed mode, thereby enabling deployment in a wide range of network environments without requiring network topology modifications.

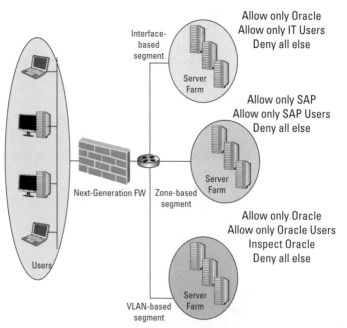

Figure 5-1: Network segmentation and security zones.

Many different technologies can be used to segment the network, but when looking at segmentation as a way to isolate the sensitive data or critical infrastructure, several key requirements need to be taken into account.

 ✔ **Flexibility.** To segment the network for security purposes may sometimes require the modification of the network architecture, a task that most companies will avoid if at all possible. The ability to segment a network using IP address ranges, VLANs, physical interfaces, or a combination thereof, is paramount.

 ✔ **Policy-based security.** Policies must be based on the identity of users and the applications in use — not just IP addresses, ports, and protocols. Without knowing and controlling exactly who (users) and what (applications and content) has access within a segment, sensitive data may be exposed to applications and users that can easily bypass controls based on IP addresses, ports, and protocols.

 ✔ **Performance.** Segmentation means applying in-depth security policies in a network location that is typically business-critical, high-volume traffic. This means it is critical that the solution delivering the secure segment operate at multi-gigabit speeds with very high session rates and minimal latency.

Addressing Mobile and Remote Users

Another technical limitation for traditional firewalls is providing visibility and control for users that are mobile or remote, beyond the perimeter established by enterprise firewalls. The challenge for next-generation firewalls in this case is to deliver a solution that provides the same degree of protection and application enablement received by users on the local network without having to manage a completely independent set of policies. Another major challenge is to avoid the limitations and disadvantages associated with the current crop of solutions in this area, including

✔ **Endpoint security suites.** Distribution and installation are often problematic, while overloaded feature sets typically create challenges in terms of client-side performance, resource requirements, and ongoing administration.

✔ **Cloud or CPE-based proxies.** Associated Web services and products typically focus on a narrow traffic stream (for example, port 80/HTTP only), can have a limited set of services/countermeasures (such as URL or malware filtering only), and — because they rely on a proxy architecture — often have to allow many applications to bypass their filters in order to avoid breaking them.

✔ **Backhaul via VPN technology.** Whether it's IPSec or SSL-based makes little difference. There is an inevitable bump in latency as client traffic is directed back to one of a few central sites where the VPN gateways are typically located. Of even greater concern, however, is the lack of application visibility and control of the head-end devices that are subsequently used to identify and filter this traffic.

In comparison, a solution that relies on a persistent client that can be installed on demand provides a better alternative. Like the VPN-based approach, remote traffic is sent over a secure tunnel. The difference in this case is that the connection is automatically made to the nearest next-generation firewall — whether it's deployed at one of an organization's hub facilities, out in a regional or branch office location, or as part of a public/private cloud implementation. The latency impact is thus minimized, and the user's session is protected and controlled by the full portfolio of application-, user-, and content-oriented identification and inspection technologies — exactly as if the user were operating on the local network instead of remotely. The net result is an easy-to-implement solution that provides remote and mobile users with the same degree of application enablement and protection as their in-office counterparts.

Chapter 6

Ten Evaluation Criteria for Next-Generation Firewalls

In This Chapter

▶ Knowing what features to look for in a next-generation firewall!

*T*his chapter gives you a few answers to look for from the vendors you are considering, once you've developed your RFP. *Note:* If you haven't yet developed an RFP to define your next-generation firewall requirements, go to Chapter 5 — go directly to Chapter 5, do not pass Go, do not collect 200 dollars!

Identify Applications, Not Ports

Identifying an application as soon as the firewall sees it, irrespective of port, protocol, SSL encryption, or other evasive tactics, provides the greatest amount of application knowledge and the best opportunity for policy control.

Finally, it is important that the next-generation firewall have an extensive library of application signatures installed on the device, in order to avoid any latency issues that may occur with a hosted or "in-the-cloud" database. The library should be regularly updated with new application signatures from the vendor or through a subscription service, and signature updates should be automated (if desired).

Application identification is at the core of traffic classification on NGFWs. It is intelligent, scalable, and extensible, and always on — across all ports and on all traffic. If this isn't true, it isn't a next-generation firewall.

Identify Users, Not IP Addresses

Seamless integration with enterprise directory services (such as Active Directory, LDAP, and eDirectory) enables administrators to tie network activity to users and groups, not just IP addresses. When used with application- and content identification technologies, IT organizations can leverage user and group information for visibility, policy creation, forensic investigation and reporting on application, threat, Web surfing, and data transfer activity.

User identification helps address the challenge of using IP addresses to monitor and control the activity of specific users — something that was once fairly simple, but has become difficult as enterprises moved to an Internet-centric model.

Compounding the visibility problem is an increasingly mobile enterprise, where employees access the network from virtually anywhere around the world, internal wireless networks re-assign IP addresses as users move from zone to zone, and network users are not always company employees. The result is that the IP address is now an inadequate mechanism for monitoring and controlling user activity.

Look for the following techniques in NGFWs to verify and maintain the user-to-IP address relationship and accurately identify users:

- **Login monitoring:** Login activity is monitored to correlate an IP address to user and group info when a user logs in to the domain.

- **End-station polling:** Each active PC is polled to verify IP address information to maintain accurate mapping when users move around the network without reauthenticating to the domain.

- **Captive portal:** Associates user and IP address in cases where hosts are not part of the domain via a web page-based authentication form.

- **Ease of deployment:** User identification should be performed without impacting critical infrastructure. Some solutions require an agent to be installed on every domain controller in the organization, which can impact performance and significantly complicate deployment.

Identify Content, Not Packets

With employees using any application they desire and surfing the Web with impunity, it's no wonder that enterprises struggle to protect the network from threat activity. The first step in regaining control over the threat activity is to identify and control applications to reduce the unwanted or bad application activity — commonly used as threat vectors. Next, policies to control content can be implemented to complement the application usage control policies.

Content identification capabilities in a NGFW should include

✔ **Threat prevention:** Look for innovative features to address changes in the threat landscape and prevent application vulnerabilities, spyware, and viruses from penetrating the network. Examples of such features include application decoders that take streams of application data that have been reassembled and parsed, and inspect the stream for specific threat identifiers, as well as uniform threat engines and signature formats to detect and block a wide range of malware (such as viruses, spyware, and vulnerability exploits) in a single pass rather than using a separate set of scanning engines and signatures for each type of threat.

✔ **Stream-based virus scanning:** This technique begins scanning as soon as the first packets of a file are received as opposed to waiting until the entire file is loaded into memory to begin scanning. This minimizes performance and latency issues by receiving, scanning, and sending traffic to its intended destination immediately without having to buffer and then scan the file.

✔ **Vulnerability attack protection:** Application vulnerability prevention is enabled using a set of intrusion prevention system (IPS) features to block known and unknown network and application-layer vulnerability exploits, buffer overflows, denial-of-service (DoS) attacks, and port scans from compromising and damaging enterprise information resources. IPS mechanisms include

- Protocol decoders and anomaly detection

- Stateful pattern matching

- Statistical anomaly detection

- Heuristic-based analysis

- Block invalid or malformed packets

- IP defragmentation and TCP reassembly

- Custom vulnerability and spyware signatures

Traffic is normalized to eliminate invalid and malformed packets, while TCP reassembly and IP defragmentation is performed to ensure the utmost accuracy and protection despite any attack evasion techniques.

✔ **URL filtering:** The URL filtering database should be on-box to reduce latency issues associated with hosted databases. Customization features should include the ability to create custom URL categories and to create granular policies for specific groups and users that can allow, block, or warn then allow, access to Web sites.

✔ **File and data filtering:** Data filtering enables administrators to implement policies that reduce the risks associated with the transfer of unauthorized files/data.

- **File blocking by type:** Control the flow of a wide range of file types by looking deep within the payload to identify the file type (as opposed to looking only at the file extension).

- **Data filtering:** Control the transfer of sensitive data patterns such as credit card and social security numbers in application content or attachments.

- **File transfer function control:** Control the file transfer functionality within an individual application, allowing application use yet preventing undesired inbound or outbound file transfer.

All of the preceding! The next six features described are much less technical, but nonetheless important.

Visibility

Next-generation firewalls give IT administrators actionable data presented in an effective manner — the ability to quickly and easily view specific, detailed application, user, and content information is invaluable.

Control

A robust next-generation firewall solution provides granular application usage control policies, such as any combination of

- ✔ Allow or deny
- ✔ Allow certain application functions and apply traffic shaping
- ✔ Allow but scan
- ✔ Decrypt and inspect
- ✔ Allow for certain users or groups

Performance

In-line NGFWs must perform advanced network security functions that are computationally intensive — and they must do so in real-time while introducing little or no latency. A next-generation firewall needs to be capable of handling multi-gigabit traffic flows using high-speed function-specific processors on purpose-built platforms. Ideally, to ensure availability of management and packet processing, the management plane and control plane should be separate.

Flexibility

Networking flexibility helps ensure compatibility with virtually any organization's computing environment. Enabling implementation without the need for redesign or reconfiguration depends on supporting a wide range of networking features and options, such as:

- ✔ 802.1q and port-based VLANs
- ✔ Trunked ports
- ✔ Transparent mode
- ✔ Dynamic routing protocols (such as OSPF and BGP)
- ✔ IPv6 support

- ✔ IPSec and SSL VPN support
- ✔ High-capacity interfaces and multiple, mixed modes (such as tap, Layer 1, Layer 2, and Layer 3)

Reliability

Reliability helps ensure nonstop operations and entails features such as:

- ✔ Active-passive and/or active-active failover
- ✔ State and configuration synchronization
- ✔ Redundant components (such as dual power supplies)

Scalability

Scalability is primarily dependent on having solid management capabilities (including centralized device and policy management, and synchronization among devices) and high-performance hardware, but can also be facilitated by support for virtual systems, where one physical firewall can be configured to act as many.

Manageability

Manageability is an important characteristic to look for in a next-generation firewall. A sophisticated solution that is too difficult to administer and maintain will inevitably fail to achieve maximum effectiveness and even risks being deployed in an incorrect — and insecure — manner. Important management capabilities include

- ✔ Local and remote management
- ✔ Centralized management
- ✔ Role-based administration
- ✔ Automatic signature updates
- ✔ Real-time monitoring of device status and security events
- ✔ Robust logging and customizable reporting

Glossary

Ares: Ares Galaxy is an open source P2P file-sharing program for Microsoft Windows, written in Delphi. Proponents for the software claim that it is able to download quickly, has a better and more complete search function than other file-sharing programs, and connects quickly.

AV: Anti-virus.

BearShare: BearShare is a P2P file-sharing application.

BGP: Border Gateway Protocol.

BitTorrent: BitTorrent is a P2P file-sharing communications protocol that distributes large amounts of data widely without the original distributor incurring the costs of hardware, hosting, and bandwidth resources. Instead, each user supplies pieces of the data to newer recipients, reducing the cost and burden on any given individual source.

Boface: Boface is a worm that tricks Facebook users into purchasing a fake anti-virus program after downloading and installing malware to their computer.

CPE: Customer-premises equipment or customer-provided equipment.

eMule: eMule is a P2P file-sharing application that features direct exchange of sources between client nodes, fast recovery of corrupted downloads, and the use of a credit system to reward frequent uploaders. It transmits data in zlib-compressed form to save bandwidth.

FastTrack: FastTrack is a P2P protocol.

Fbaction: Fbaction is a phishing attack targeted against Facebook users.

FINRA: Financial Industry Regulatory Authority.

FTP: File Transfer Protocol.

Gbridge: Gbridge establishes a VPN tunnel inside of a Google Gtalk instant messaging session (Gbridge is not a Google application). A Gbridge user can then connect to multiple PCs that are logged in under the same Gtalk user account.

Gnutella: As of December 2005, Gnutella was the third-most-popular Internet file sharing network. Popular clients for Gnutella include Limewire, Morpheus, and BearShare.

Gpass: Gpass is an Internet anti-jamming product widely used in China to overcome Internet censorship. It effectively protects user privacy and online safety by providing a secure Internet access mechanism.

HA: Highly available or high availability.

HIPAA: Health Insurance Portability and Accountability Act.

HTTP: Hypertext Transfer Protocol.

HTTPS: Hypertext Transfer Protocol over SSL/TLS.

IM: Instant Messenger.

IPSec: Internet Protocol Security (IPSec) is a protocol suite for protecting communications over IP networks using authentication and encryption.

Kazaa: Kazaa is a P2P file-sharing application that uses the FastTrack protocol.

Koobface: Koobface is a worm that tricks Facebook users into downloading and installing a fake update of the Adobe Flash player. Among other things, Koobface attempts to collect sensitive information such as credit card numbers from an infected PC.

LDAP: Lightweight Directory Access Protocol.

Limewire: Limewire is an open-source P2P application.

Mariposa: Mariposa is a botnet that was built with the computer virus known as "Butterfly Bot" and is estimated to have infected between 8 and 12 million PCs worldwide. The Mariposa Botnet steals passwords for Web sites and financial institutions, launches denial of service attacks, and spreads viruses.

Mediafire: Mediafire is a free and unlimited file and image hosting Web site. The service is available for free and allows users to upload files of up to 100 MB.

Morpheus: Morpheus is a P2P application.

MS-RPC: Microsoft Remote Procedure Call is a communications protocol used on Microsoft Windows networks.

Orkut: Social networking site owned and operated by Google.

OSI: Open Systems Interconnection model. The seven-layer reference model for networks. The layers are Physical, Data Link, Network, Transport, Session, Presentation, and Application.

OSPF: Open Shortest Path First.

P2P: Peer-to-Peer.

PCI DSS: Payment Card Industry Data Security Standard.

QoS: Quality of Service.

RIP: Routing Information Protocol.

Skype: Skype is an application that allows users to make telephone calls over the Internet. Additional features include instant messaging, file transfer, and video conferencing.

SMB: Server Message Block is an application-layer protocol also known as Common Internet File System (CIFS).

SMTP: Simple Mail Transfer Protocol.

SSH: Secure Shell is a set of standards and an associated network protocol that allows establishing a secure channel between a local and a remote computer.

SSL/TLS: Secure Sockets Layer/Transport Layer Security. A transport layer protocol that provides session-based encryption and authentication for secure communication between clients and servers on the Internet.

Stateful inspection: Also known as dynamic packet filtering; maintains the status of active connections through the firewall to dynamically allow inbound replies to outbound connections.

TCP: Transmission Control Protocol.

Teamviewer: Teamviewer provides remote control of PCs over the Internet, allowing a user to instantly take control over a computer anywhere on the Internet, even through firewalls.

UDP: User Datagram Protocol.

UltraSurf: UltraSurf implements a proxy with complete transparency and a high level of encryption that enables users to browse any Web site freely. It is used heavily in countries with Internet censorship.

URL: Uniform Resource Locator.

VLAN: Virtual Local Area Network.

VoIP: Voice over Internet Protocol.

VPN: Virtual Private Network.

zlib: zlib is a software library used for data compression.